HANGOVER CURES

HANGOVER CURES

BEN REED

photography by WILLIAM LINGWOOD

RYLAND
PETERS
& SMALL

LONDON NEW YORK

First published in the
United States in 2005
by Ryland Peters & Small, Inc.
519 Broadway
5th Floor
New York, NY 10012
www.rylandpeters.com

10 9 8 7 6 5 4 3 2 1

Text © Ben Reed 2005
Design and photographs
© Ryland Peters & Small 2005
Some of the recipes in this book
have been previously published
by Ryland Peters & Small.

ISBN 1 84172 972 8

Printed in China

Senior Designer **Paul Tilby**
Editor **Miriam Hyslop**
Production **Gavin Bradshaw**

Art Director **Gabriella Le Grazie**
Publishing Director **Alison Starling**

contents

introduction

Let's face it, the occasional hangover, for those of us who enjoy a tipple, is a certainty in life. But why do we continue to punish ourselves? Surely, in this day and age, we must have developed the technology to counteract the nausea, lethargy, dry mouth, and nagging headaches we experience with a hangover? Sadly not. While the following chapters may help ease your suffering (or, at least, attach a crooked smile to your pained expression), quite simply the only way to truly cure a hangover is not to drink too much the night before.

myths

I'm not going to beat around the bush—the following "cures" don't work. Stop tormenting yourselves.

A cup of coffee in the morning This old villain may well help to wake you up, but it contains caffeine (a diuretic), which will increase dehydration and irritate your stomach further. If you need a stimulant, try ginseng. If you are a regular coffee drinker, however, you may want to administer a small dose of caffeine—there's no need to suffer from two drug withdrawals at the same time!

The hair of the dog that bit you Some more alcohol will take away your pain but will possibly return it two-fold the next day. For me, however, anything that will ease my suffering for even a second is worth a try. (When hung over, I don't read the small print, my eyes find it hard enough to stay open as it is, I don't care that it's not going to last.)

Sex I really don't enjoy being the killjoy here, but sex just isn't the cure it really should be. Can you imagine if it was, though...?

cures from around the world

You've heard of them and you've probably tried a few of them out of sheer desperation. The old wives' tale is never more in its element than when applied to the hangover. Here are a few of my favorites from around the world:

If you are in **France,** drink thick, hot onion soup the morning after.

In **Switzerland** they rely on a shot of brandy with a hint of peppermint. (Typical Swiss, always on hand with a brandy!)

If you find yourself hung over in **Russia**, you'd probably be recommended heavily salted cucumber juice and black bread soaked in water (I can see what they're getting at, but cucumber juice...?).

A glass of heavy cream would be the solution in **Norway.**

If, by some strange twist of fate (or at a bachelor party gone horribly wrong), you wake up the worse for wear in **Outer Mongolia**, you might wish for home when presented with a pickled sheep's eye in a glass of tomato juice to cure your ills.

You've got to love those Puerto Ricans for one of the least mettle-testing cures—when in **Puerto Rico**, rub a lemon into the armpit of your drinking arm.

The cure from **Haiti** must take pride of place on the back bar in the hangover hostelry from hell. You, too, can cure your hangover by simply sticking thirteen black-headed-pins into the cork of the bottle that got you that way. Not a lot of draft-beer drinkers in Haiti, then!

before, during, & after

The answer to the question "What causes a hangover?" is a complex one. There is more than one reason for all that pain. Most hangovers are caused by a combination of dehydration (lack of fluids in the body), the loss of sugars and salts, and poisoning of the system with alcohol—or, more precisely, the impurities in alcohol.

You can never really know when one is going to creep up on you and, once it's there, how to deal with it. However, help is at hand. Here are some ways to avoid a hangover just by being a bit clever (and, let's face it, none of us are particularly good at this while under the influence), so read carefully.

Before you even leave the house—that's right, while you're still sober—have something to eat
This slows absorption of alcohol. Carbs and fatty foods are best. If you can't find the time to eat, drink a glass of milk at least. If you get the chance to eat something during the evening, do.

Have a glass of water after each alcoholic drink
Water keeps your body hydrated. When you drink alcohol, its diuretic qualities mean that your body expels more liquid than you drink. The body requires water to function and, if various organs within it are deprived, they will steal it from wherever they can, including the brain (see where I'm going here?). The brain doesn't actually feel pain, but, when it starts shrinking due to loss of fluid, filaments connecting the outside membranes to the inner skull start to stretch and this is what gives you the gnawing pain in your head in the morning. Dehydration caused from increased alcohol intake makes your brain shrink. Now will you listen to me?

Stick to one drink an hour to give your body a chance to absorb the alcohol cumulatively
The body only has the facility to process roughly one ounce (a half-jigger) of alcohol an hour (this varies depending on gender, body size, tolerance levels, etc.). On a serious note, this rule of thumb is well worth remembering for those of us who may have to drive to work early in the morning after a late night.

Don't mix different types of alcohol It takes the body longer to recognize and metabolize each individual type of alcohol.

If you "mix it up," remember the rules Beer before liquor, never sicker. Liquor before beer, no fear. Beer then wine, feel fine. Wine then beer, feel queer. Confused? Me, too.

Stick to light-colored liquors Dark liquors contain more congeners (the impurities that give alcohol taste), which will have a rousing effect on the drum solo that is about to kick off in your head.

Remember, carbonated drinks affect you faster The bubbles help the body absorb the alcohol at an increased rate.

Drink premium liquors The more expensive the alcohol, invariably, the better its method of distillation (the production method that helps to remove the congeners).

Avoid too many sweet drinks (like piña coladas) Not only do they make you look like a bit of a jerk, but the sweet flavors often hide the taste of alcohol, giving you an unrealistic view on how much you are drinking.

Drink a pint of lightly-salted water before going to bed Frequent visits to the toilet will result in the loss of salt as well as water. Salts contain potassium and sodium, which are essential for maintaining a healthy body. If you are determined to stave off the pain, and you have a strong stomach, drinking a large glass of lightly salted water before going to bed will help (and another would help even more). I recommend trying this the night before, as it's not going to get any easier the next day.

Eat something sweet before bed Alcohol attacks the glycogen that is stored in the body. It breaks it down to glucose, which is washed out of the body when you visit the restroom. When this energy source is depleted, you will feel heavily fatigued in the morning.

Try a banana, honey, and peanut butter sandwich The banana and honey contain potassium and glucose. Bananas are also high in magnesium, which can relax the pounding blood vessels in your head, and contain natural antacids to help soothe your gnarled stomach. And why peanut butter...? Not too sure, but it sure tastes great!

Have a long, hot powerful shower I'm digging into the pockets of personal experience here, but a shower, especially one with massaging jets, often helps. Aim the jets on your neck or anywhere else you feel tense, and your muscles will relax, relieving tension. This is especially useful for those of us who have a penchant for subjecting our body (and pride) to a turn on the dance floor! If that's too hectic, try a hot bath!

Take milk thistle extract On a love-your-liver tip, this herb is quite butch when it comes to limiting the damage done by free radicals.

Go for a brisk walk Increased oxygen intake can improve the metabolic rate, thus increasing the speed at which toxins are broken down within the body.

Drink isotonic sports drinks These are typically used by sports persons to replace salts and sugars sweated out during exercise, which is exactly why they are good for hangovers! Try to avoid the carbonated isotonic drinks, though, as they will only bloat your stomach.

hair of the dog

"The hair of the dog that bit you" will only take the edge off your hangover and will inevitably make you feel worse the next day. Choose your pick-me-up carefully, though, and you can certainly weather the storm just that little bit longer. Bartender, a Stinger with a Red Eye chaser, if you please.

The Corpse Reviver is very much a hair-of-the-dog type of hangover cure. It will either ease your suffering or send you straight back to bed.

corpse reviver

1 OZ. CALVADOS (APPLE BRANDY)
1 OZ. VERMOUTH ROSSO
1 OZ. BRANDY
ORANGE SLICE, TO GARNISH

Shake the ingredients over ice and strain into a frosted martini glass. Garnish with a slice of orange and serve.

prairie oyster

A DASH OF OLIVE OIL

1 EGG YOLK

A DASH OF TABASCO SAUCE

2 DASHES OF WORCESTERSHIRE SAUCE

SALT AND PEPPER

2 DASHES OF VINEGAR OR LEMON JUICE

Not for the faint-hearted, the Prairie Oyster is one of those drinks you have to try at least once in your life.

Rinse a cocktail glass with the olive oil and carefully add the egg yolk. Add the seasoning to taste and serve. This cocktail is best drunk quickly, in one (for obvious reasons!).

The Stormy Weather is well qualified to treat your hangover, with its good measure of Fernet Branca, a very bitter digestif that is often used on its own as a hangover cure.

stormy weather

1 OZ. FERNET BRANCA

1 OZ. DRY VERMOUTH

2 DASHES OF CRÈME DE MENTHE

Shake all the ingredients over ice, strain into a small highball glass filled with ice and garnish with a sprig of mint.

vodka stinger

The Vodka Stinger gives your mouth a certain minty freshness that will at least banish any lingering night-before tastes.

2 OZ. VODKA

A LARGE DASH OF CRÈME DE MENTHE (WHITE)

Shake the ingredients over ice and strain into a martini glass.

pick me up

Fernet Branca was the only legitimate alcohol available in the USA during Prohibition, due to its amazing restorative properties.

1 OZ. FERNET BRANCA

1 OZ. SWEET VERMOUTH

2 DASHES OF ANGOSTURA BITTERS

Build all ingredients into a highball glass over ice and stir gently.

red eye

Yet another cocktail with an egg in it!

EQUAL PARTS BEER AND TOMATO JUICE

AN EGG

Add equal quantities of beer and tomato juice to a Pilsner glass. Crack an egg into the glass and serve.

strawberry flip

Flips are considered restorative, thanks to the egg yolk. I've added strawberries for those of you that are a little squeamish at the prospect of drinking egg.

4 FRESH STRAWBERRIES

2 OZ. CRÈME DE FRAISE

1 TABLESPOON SIMPLE SYRUP

AN EGG YOLK

Muddle the strawberries in a mixing glass and add the rest of the ingredients. Strain into a martini glass or a brandy snifter and serve.

hair of the dog

The fructose in the honey will replace lost sugars. The heavy cream should calm your stomach (try equal parts cream and milk for a gentler version), and the Scotch will ease your headache for as long as it takes you to get back in to bed!

2 OZ. SCOTCH WHISKY

1 OZ. HEAVY CREAM

1 OZ. CLEAR HONEY

Shake all ingredients and strain over ice into a rocks glass.

bellini

The Bellini originated in Harry's Bar in Venice in the 1940s. Although there are many variations on this recipe, there is one golden rule for the perfect Bellini—always use fresh, ripe peaches to make the peach juice.

1/2 FRESH PEACH, SKINNED

1/2 OZ. CRÈME DE PÊCHE

A DASH OF PEACH BITTERS (OPTIONAL)

CHAMPAGNE, TO TOP UP

PEACH BALL, TO GARNISH

Puree the peach in a blender and add to a champagne flute. Pour in the crème de pêche and the peach bitters, and gently top up with champagne, stirring carefully and continuously. Garnish with a peach ball in the bottom of the glass, then serve.

mimosa

It is thought that Alfred Hitchcock invented this drink in an old San Francisco eatery called Jack's, sometime in the 1940s, for a group of friends suffering from hangovers.

FRESH ORANGE JUICE, TO TOP UP

1/2 GLASS OF CHAMPAGNE

Pour the orange juice over half a flute full of champagne and stir gently.

salty mexican dog

This is a tequila variation on the Salty Dog, traditionally made with vodka. It's a simple combination that can cut through the fog of any hangover with its trinity of grapefruit, salt, and tequila.

SALT, FOR THE GLASS

2 OZ. TEQUILA

8 OZ. GRAPEFRUIT JUICE

LIME WEDGE, TO GARNISH

Pour the tequila into a salt-rimmed highball glass filled with ice. Top up with the grapefruit juice, garnish with a lime wedge, and serve with two straws.

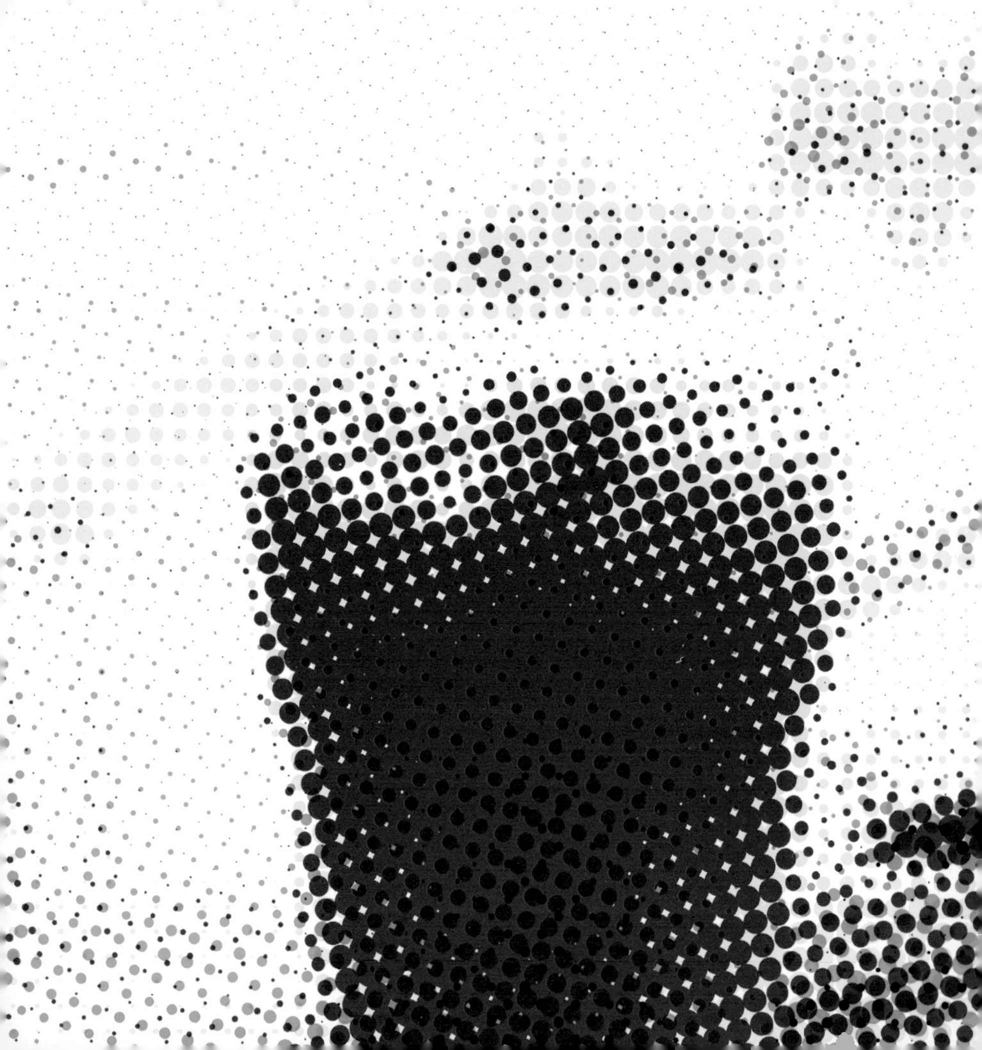

bloody marys

I'm a sucker for a Bloody Mary. I'm even happy with a Bloody Shame—this drink's not about the alcohol; rather the collective spices and the juice. If you don't spice your Bloody Mary, it becomes simply a vodka and tomato juice. If you ain't sweating (sorry, ladies—perspiring!), you've been served the wrong drink.

The Bloody Mary is for those who feel a little worse for wear and can't face food. It's the perfect solution: a meal in a glass.

bloody mary

2 OZ. VODKA

10 OZ. TOMATO JUICE

PINCH OF GROUND BLACK PEPPER

2 DASHES OF WORCESTERSHIRE SAUCE

2 DASHES OF TABASCO SAUCE

2 DASHES OF FRESH LEMON JUICE

BARSPOON HORSERADISH

CELERY STALK, TO GARNISH

Shake all the ingredients over ice and strain into a highball filled with ice. Garnish with a celery stalk.

To make a Bloody Shame, simply leave out the vodka.

bloody maria

If ever I find the need to seek solace in a hangover cure, the Bloody Maria is a worthy adversary to the Mary. Where the vodka in a Mary thins the mixture, the tequila in a Maria binds the ingredients.

2 OZ. GOLD TEQUILA

1/2 OZ. FRESH LIME JUICE

8 OZ. TOMATO JUICE

5 DASHES OF TABASCO SAUCE

5 DASHES OF WORCESTERSHIRE SAUCE

PINCH OF SEA SALT OR KOSHER SALT

PINCH OF GROUND BLACK PEPPER

PINCH OF CELERY SALT

LIME WEDGE, TO GARNISH

CELERY STALK, TO GARNISH

Add all the ingredients to a shaker filled with ice. Shake sharply and strain into a highball glass filled with ice. Garnish with a lime wedge and celery.

Red Snapper was the name given to the Bloody Mary in the 1940s, when the original was deemed too risqué. I've taken the name but changed the format.

red snapper

2 OZ. GIN

3 OZ. TOMATO JUICE

4 DASHES OF TABASCO SAUCE

PINCH OF CELERY SALT

2 DASHES OF LEMON JUICE

PINCH OF GROUND BLACK PEPPER

4 DASHES OF WORCESTERSHIRE SAUCE

BLACK PEPPER OR LEMON ZEST, TO GARNISH

Add all the ingredients to a shaker filled with ice, shake sharply, then strain into a frosted martini glass. Garnish with a sprinkling of black pepper or lemon zest.

gazpacho

This savory drink might sound like a strange choice, but trust me, as it works! The Gazpacho came about when a friend and I were out for brunch and were looking for a change of drink from the Bloody Mary. Gazpacho was on the menu, so we put two and two together, et voilà!

2 OZ. PEPPER VODKA

BLACK PEPPER, TO TASTE

8 OZ. GAZPACHO SOUP

CHOPPED HERBS, TO GARNISH

Shake all the ingredients really hard with ice and strain into a martini glass. Sprinkle some chopped herbs over it to garnish.

bloody caesar

Bloody aficionados swear by this variation on the Mary. By simply using clamato (a mixture of clam and tomato) juice instead of just tomato, you have a slightly sweeter, meatier-tasting drink. It is spiced, though, so temperance is required when adding your seasoning!

2 OZ. VODKA

8 OZ. CLAMATO JUICE

HOT PEPPER SAUCE, TO TASTE

A DASH OF LEMON JUICE

SALT AND PEPPER

Add all ingredients to a shaker filled with ice. Shake sharply and strain into a highball glass filled with ice.

bloody maru

A gentle, elegant Bloody from Japan. Don't overdo the spices, as you'll overwhelm the sake.

4 OZ. SAKE

8 OZ. CLAMATO JUICE

PINCH OF WASABI

A DASH OF SOY SAUCE

Add all ingredients to a shaker filled with ice, shake gently and strain into highball (or appropriate glass). Then garnish with a California roll on a chopstick.

This might be a drink served in shot glasses, but it's not meant to be drunk quickly—quite the opposite. The tequila should be served at room temperature and sipped alternately with the tomato juice and orange, which is chilled and flavored with lime juice. The gold tequila combines very effectively with the tomato juice, its oily aftertaste making it more of a stalker than a chaser! This cocktail doesn't disguise the taste of any of its components—it just emphasizes their great working relationship.

the sangrita

2 OZ. GOLD TEQUILA

1 OZ. TOMATO JUICE (CHILLED)

1 OZ. ORANGE JUICE

A DASH OF FRESH LIME JUICE

A DASH OF GRENADINE

A SPRINKLE OF BLACK PEPPER

Pour the tequila (unchilled) into a shot glass. Add the tomato juice to another shot glass and mix in the lemon juice and pepper. The two drinks should be sipped alternately.

bullshot

I find the Bullshot quite comforting. It isn't necessary to spice this one as heavily as a Bloody Mary, but I find celery salt works well.

1 1/2 OZ. VODKA

5 OZ. BEEF BOUILLON

SALT AND PEPPER AND CELERY SALT, TO TASTE

A DASH OF LEMON JUICE (OPTIONAL)

CELERY STALK, TO GARNISH

Add all ingredients to a shaker filled with ice. Shake sharply and strain into a highball glass filled with ice, then garnish with a celery stalk.

juices

As much it goes against the grain for the die-hard bartender, such as myself, there is a whole world of mixology to explore outside my world of bitters, fortifieds, and spirits. Juice not only boosts your sugar levels but also replaces some of the lost nutrients caused by alcohol consumption. Fresh fruit juices have undeniably restorative values.

The Liver Recovery is, as the name suggests, a drink that contains all the necessary goodness to restore an ailing liver without having to resort to the milk thistle pills. Between them, strawberries, bananas, and apples contain more nutrients and healing properties than I could fit on this page. And, even better, the drink tastes great!

liver recovery

6 FRESH STRAWBERRIES

2 GREEN APPLES

1 BANANA

Peel, core, top, and tail the assembled fruits, as necessary. Put each of them through a juicer, collecting the resulting juice. Add the juices to a blender filled with one scoop of crushed ice. Blend and pour into a small highball glass.

virgin banana colada

RIPE BANANA
(RESERVE A SLICE, TO GARNISH)

3/4 OZ. COCONUT CREAM

2 TEASPOONS HEAVY CREAM

5 OZ. PINEAPPLE JUICE

This one works both as a meal and a drink! To make it alcoholic, add a large measure of Bailey's, which adds a kick and makes the drink even more viscous.

Add all the ingredients to a blender with a scoop of crushed ice and blend for 20 seconds. Pour into a hurricane glass and garnish with a banana slice. Serve with two straws.

The Pussy Foot fulfils all the basic criteria for this category—refreshing, rehydrating, and, most importantly, packed full of nutrients. The combination of potassium and vitamin C should help you feel better in no time.

pussy foot

3 OZ. FRESH PINEAPPLE JUICE

3 OZ. FRESH CRANBERRY JUICE

3 OZ. FRESH ORANGE JUICE

3 OZ. FRESH GRAPEFRUIT JUICE

A DASH OF GRENADINE

2 DASHES OF FRESH LEMON JUICE

Shake the ingredients well over ice and strain into a highball glass filled with ice.

banana
blitz

Easy to make, no fiddly peeling or trembling hands slicing fruit. The orange juice and the banana are for vitamin C, and potassium and the strawberries for flavor, if nothing else!

1 CUP ORANGE JUICE

1 CUP HULLED AND QUARTERED
FRESH STRAWBERRIES

2 PEELED BANANAS

Add all ingredients to a blender, blend until smooth and serve in a highball glass.

smooth
as silk

I've included this one as it helps cancel out the effects of alcohol on your sleep pattern. Alcohol disrupts sleep (which is one of the few things that will truly cure a hangover!).

2 CUPS BLACKBERRIES

1 RIPE BANANA

WHOLE APPLE

Blend all ingredients and pour into a highball glass. Drink 45 minutes before going to sleep.

When you're peeling the fruit for this restorative punch, leave on a little of the bitter pith and add it to the drink. If your lemon is thin-skinned, you can leave the skin on, too. The pith contains the tonic's main bioflavonoids, which help build up the immune system.

grapefruit glitz

2 GRAPEFRUIT

2 ORANGES

1 LEMON

Peel the fruit. Add all the ingredients to a blender with crushed ice, and blend. Pour into a highball glass and serve.

carrot, apple, and ginger

No fancy name for this one, but the carrot contains amazingly healthy nutrients called carotenoids. Ginger has been used for centuries as a cure-all and will soothe types of nausea and sickness. Apples contain a huge amount of vitamin A and C. Add a little honey to sweeten.

3 LARGE PEELED CARROTS (TOPPED AND TAILED)

2 SMALL APPLES (UNPEELED)

1 THUMBNAIL FRESH GINGER

Push the carrots and apples through a juicer, collecting the resulting juice. Grate the ginger into the mixture and serve in a highball glass.

This blend of juices will boost the immune system. But, unlike that spoon of cod-liver oil adminstered at school, this one actually tastes good.

back to school

Put all of the ingredients into a blender. Add ice and blend for 20 seconds. Pour into a highball glass and serve.

3 PEELED TANGERINES

1/2 PINEAPPLE SLICED WITH SKIN

3/4 CUP BLACK CURRANTS

1 PEELED BANANA

A SMALL CARTON YOGURT

1/2 TABLESPOON HONEY

10 DROPS OF ECHINACEA EXTRACT

life saver

The carrots and the radishes in the Life Saver are both great liver cleansers.

6 PEELED CARROTS (TOPPED AND TAILED)

4 RADISHES (WITH LEAVES, IF POSSIBLE)

2 WHOLE APPLES

Blend all ingredients together. Pour into a hurricane or highball glass and serve.

index

conversion chart

Measures have been rounded up or down slightly to make measuring easier. The key is to keep ingredients in ratio.

Imperial	Metric
½ oz.	10–12.5 ml
1 oz. (single)	25 ml
2 oz. (double)	50 ml